MOMENTS OF INSIGHT
WORKBOOK

Neil Tumber

With illustrations by

Amara Piparia-Lea

MOMENTS OF INSIGHT - WORKBOOK

Text Copyright © Neil Tumber 2018

Illustrations Copyright © Amara Piparia-Lea

Neil Tumber has asserted his right under the Copyright, Designs and Patents Act 1988 to be identified as the author of this work

Amara Piparia-Lea has asserted her right under the Copyright, Designs and Patents Act 1988 to be identified as the illustrator of this work

This book is sold subject to the condition that it shall not, by way of trade or otherwise, be lent, resold, hired out, or otherwise circulated without the publisher's prior consent in any form of binding or cover other than that in which it is purchased and without a similar condition, including this condition, being imposed on the subsequent purchaser

ISBN: 9781794604636
Imprint: Independently published

Contents

Story	Principle	
A fire-side chat	Be ready to learn wherever you are	Page 2
At the seaside	Build on each other's ideas	Page 4
Family picnic	Offer the skills you have	Page 6
Playing rugby	Develop your unique skills	Page 8
My first project	Keep team success in focus	Page 10
The go-cart	Don't assume you have all the answers	Page 12
Cooking dinner	Focus on the result	Page 14
Preparing for holiday	Careful planning leads to success	Page 16
Voyage in a submarine	Ensure you understand the basics	Page 18
Fifteen-minute meetings	Prepare to be effective	Page 20
Getting lost	Mapping your project gives you direction	Page 22
Asking for help	Don't struggle by yourself: just ask	Page 24
Broken squares	Look for safe ways to learn	Page 26
A better fire	Don't try to do everything yourself	Page 28
Team outing	Encourage people to share their talents	Page 30
Putting it all together	Working as a team	Page 32

MOMENTS OF INSIGHT - WORKBOOK

Introduction

The concept behind our book, "Moments of Insight", is that we all experience many different ways of working with others. As we react to new situations or new people sometimes, we find it easy to join the team and make a positive contribution. On other occasions, it is more difficult. Often, it is because the current project or task seems similar to one in the past so we think that the same approach will work. Crucially, however, one or more factors have changed. That's when looking back on your past experience can give you clues as to how you need to behave now. Experiences from early childhood are very precious because, at that stage, you were naturally open, curious and willing to try new things.

We have created this workbook to help you reflect on the stories from, "Moments of Insight" and, in particular, to identify stories of your own that can help you become a better team member. For each story, we give you space to write your own story, to identify the key learning points and make a commitment to put that learning into practice.

To tell your own story, you need to set the scene: where were you and who was with you? Then you need to state the problem facing you or the group before relating what happened: what was said? What actions were taken and by whom? Finally, you need a conclusion: a statement of the outcome. Was the problem solved? If yes, what was the key factor in achieving that outcome. If not, can you identify why that was. We should be open to learning at all times - remember that we learn best from our mistakes.

It is very important to be as specific as you can. This is will help you really engage with each story to help you learn and then to remember the learning! The more you add details to your story, the more vivid it will be, giving you a rich learning experience.

How to use this workbook

You can use this workbook on your own or in a group.

On your own, it will be good to write your story and then take a break: do something different for a while. After the break, re-read your story and look for the key learning point. You will be surprised how often that it is not the obvious thing that made the difference to the outcome. Finally, write down an action statement to encourage you to apply that learning today.

In a group, it will be great to share your stories with each other. Ask questions. Seek understanding. Offer observations. Be ready and willing learn from each other. As when using the book on your own, look for that one thing that you will remember to do for your team.

Your action statement might be to do something different, but it might also be to carry on doing something that you already do. The important thing is to do those things that will most help your team to succeed.

MOMENTS OF INSIGHT - WORKBOOK

Now its your turn to tell the stories!

A fire-side chat

> Be ready to learn wherever you are

What was the most unusual place where you learned something new?

When did this story take place? Where were you? Who was with you?

What was the problem?

What happened?

MOMENTS OF INSIGHT - WORKBOOK

What was the outcome?

What was the key factor that led to the outcome?

As you think about this story, what will you now do for your team?

At the seaside

Build on each other's ideas

Did you create imaginary worlds with your friends?

When did this story take place? Where were you? Who was with you?

What was the problem?

What happened?

MOMENTS OF INSIGHT - WORKBOOK

What was the outcome?

What was the key factor that led to the outcome?

As you think about this story, what will you now do for your team?

Family picnic

| Offer the skills you have |

Do you get on and do what you can to help the team, or wait to be asked?

When did this story take place? Where were you? Who was with you?

What was the problem?

What happened?

MOMENTS OF INSIGHT - WORKBOOK

What was the outcome?

What was the key factor that led to the outcome?

As you think about this story, what will you now do for your team?

Playing rugby

Develop your unique skills

Think of a time when your unique skills helped your team succeed!

When did this story take place? Where were you? Who was with you?

What was the problem?

What happened?

MOMENTS OF INSIGHT - WORKBOOK

What was the outcome?

What was the key factor that led to the outcome?

As you think about this story, what will you now do for your team?

My first project

Keep team success in focus

Are you willing to give up something for the sake of the team?

When did this story take place? Where were you? Who was with you?

What was the problem?

What happened?

MOMENTS OF INSIGHT - WORKBOOK

What was the outcome?

What was the key factor that led to the outcome?

As you think about this story, what will you now do for your team?

The go-cart

Don't assume you have all the answers

When did you last receive great ideas from an unexpected source?

When did this story take place? Where were you? Who was with you?

What was the problem?

What happened?

MOMENTS OF INSIGHT - WORKBOOK

What was the outcome?

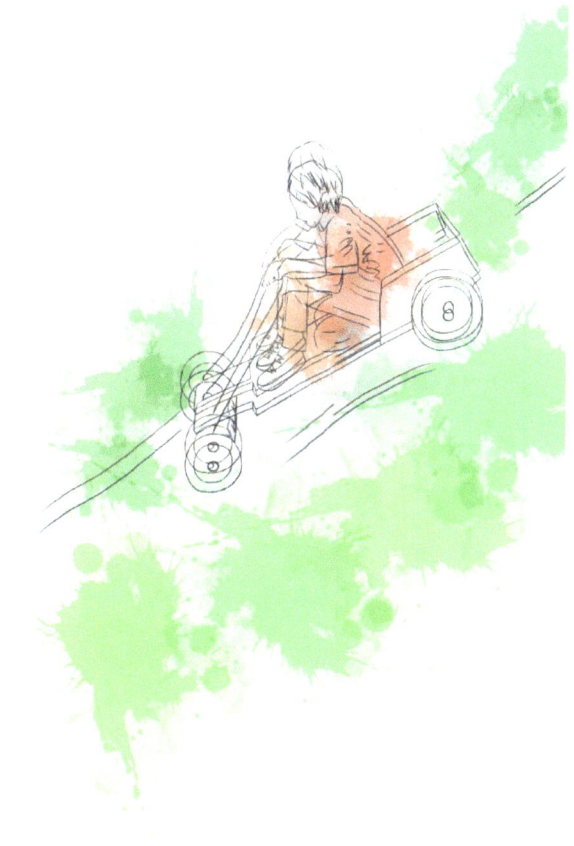

What was the key factor that led to the outcome?

As you think about this story, what will you now do for your team?

Cooking dinner

Focus on the result

Remember what fun it is to get things done!

When did this story take place? Where were you? Who was with you?

What was the problem?

What happened?

MOMENTS OF INSIGHT - WORKBOOK

What was the outcome?

What was the key factor that led to the outcome?

As you think about this story, what will you now do for your team?

Preparing for holiday

Careful planning leads to success

Compare some of your projects: does planning lead to more enjoyable action?

When did this story take place? Where were you? Who was with you?

What was the problem?

What happened?

MOMENTS OF INSIGHT - WORKBOOK

What was the outcome?

What was the key factor that led to the outcome?

As you think about this story, what will you now do for your team?

Voyage in a submarine

> **Ensure you understand the basics**

What is the essential knowledge for your place of work?

When did this story take place? Where were you? Who was with you?

What was the problem?

What happened?

MOMENTS OF INSIGHT - WORKBOOK

What was the outcome?

___

What was the key factor that led to the outcome?

As you think about this story, what will you now do for your team?

Fifteen-minute meetings

Prepare to be effective

What was your last meeting like?

When did this story take place? Where were you? Who was with you?

What was the problem?

What happened?

MOMENTS OF INSIGHT - WORKBOOK

What was the outcome?

What was the key factor that led to the outcome?

As you think about this story, what will you now do for your team?

Getting lost

| Mapping your project gives you direction |

Do you remember a time when you got lost? Did a map help you get to where you wanted to be?

When did this story take place? Where were you? Who was with you?

What was the problem?

What happened?

What was the outcome?

What was the key factor that led to the outcome?

As you think about this story, what will you now do for your team?

Asking for help

Don't struggle by yourself: just ask

Have you ever struggled to do something but when you asked found it was easy?

When did this story take place? Where were you? Who was with you?

What was the problem?

What happened?

MOMENTS OF INSIGHT - WORKBOOK

What was the outcome?

What was the key factor that led to the outcome?

As you think about this story, what will you now do for your team?

Broken squares

> Look for safe ways to learn

Has a game or activity helped you be a better team member or team leader?

When did this story take place? Where were you? Who was with you?

What was the problem?

What happened?

MOMENTS OF INSIGHT - WORKBOOK

What was the outcome?

What was the key factor that led to the outcome?

As you think about this story, what will you now do for your team?

A better fire

Don't try to do everything yourself

Do you remember to seek out skilled help?

When did this story take place? Where were you? Who was with you?

What was the problem?

What happened?

MOMENTS OF INSIGHT - WORKBOOK

What was the outcome?

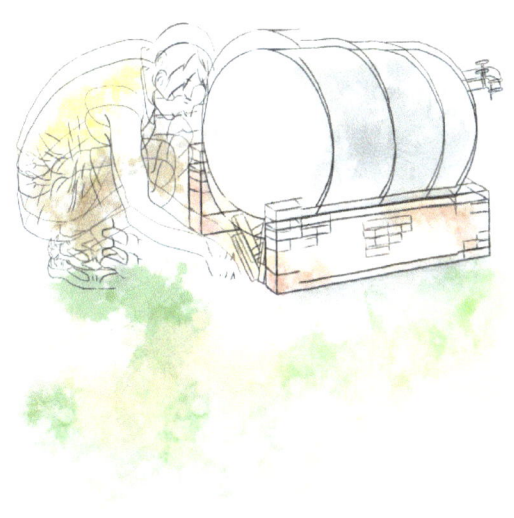

What was the key factor that led to the outcome?

As you think about this story, what will you now do for your team?

Team outing | Encourage people to share their talents

Do you have hidden talents? Could they be useful at work?

When did this story take place? Where were you? Who was with you?

What was the problem?

What happened?

MOMENTS OF INSIGHT - WORKBOOK

What was the outcome?

What was the key factor that led to the outcome?

As you think about this story, what will you now do for your team?

Putting it all together

Working as a team

What is the team achievement that you are most proud of?

When did this story take place? Where were you? Who was with you?

What was the problem?

What happened?

MOMENTS OF INSIGHT - WORKBOOK

What was the outcome?

What was the key factor that led to the outcome?

As you think about this story, what will you now do for your team?

Neil Tumber

Neil is Best Practice Leader at Thistle Management Limited: a company that promotes the identification, development and implementation of best practice in every part of a client's organization. Neil specializes in guiding leadership through the behavior and cultural change needed to establish truly open collaboration across and beyond the organization.

He was formerly Global Best Practice Leader at Bunge where he was able to demonstrate the value added when people engage in open collaboration. He has a deep faith in the ability of everyone to excel at their work and is a passionate believer that working collaboratively can make workforces happier and more creative.

He can be contacted at: www.thistlemanagement.com

Amara Piparia-Lea

Amara is studying Illustration at Hereford College of Arts. She hopes to build a freelance business after completing her BA, specialising in packaging, publications, and both adult and children's book illustration.

You can find her work on Instagram @amarapiparialeaart

www.ingramcontent.com/pod-product-compliance
Lightning Source LLC
Chambersburg PA
CBHW051933210526
45473CB00006B/2233